Social Skills for Tweens

The Ultimate Guide to Conflict Resolution, Communication, Making Friends, and More Essential Keys for Pre-Teens to Thrive in Life and Create Positive Relationships

Table of Contents

Introduction Letter to Parents

Dear Parents,

As a parent, you can probably relate to the struggle of wanting to connect with others but not knowing what to do or how to get started. If you cast your mind back to when you were a tween, you may remember several times when you didn't know how to conduct yourself. You might think of a few friendships you lost in your adolescent and teenage years because of this problem. You were never taught how to socialize, so how could you have known what to do? It also didn't help that the adults of your time may have had the simplistic idea that forcing you to hang out with others was more than enough to help you connect with them, but it wasn't.

Thankfully, you know better now. You're clearly on the lookout for your tween child because you don't want him or her to make the same mistakes you did. You have made an excellent decision by arming them with this book so they can develop the skills you wish you had mastered earlier in life.

You realize that the importance of social skills goes far beyond making friends and keeping them. You know there's more to life than book smarts, so you want to give your child emotional smarts, too. You know this is the only way you can help your little one become a well-rounded person when he or she grows up — someone who can hold their own, speak their mind, and confidently engage with the world.

So, this book has been written to help your tween master the social terrain and navigate it with ease and confidence. It is your job as a parent to give them this book and other resources to read, and more than that, to help them implement the lessons they learn.

Encourage them to ask you questions if they're unclear about something and check in regularly to see what they've learned and how they use the tools in this guide. By arming your child with the knowledge in this book and giving them your love and support, not even the sky is the limit regarding how much they can develop socially. You're doing the right thing for your child. One day, many years later, they'll look back on the day you got them this book, and they'll also thank you for it.

NOTE: Some sections involving complex emotional management techniques, such as empathy mapping or digital etiquette (both in chapter 8), might require adult guidance to ensure an understanding of them – and how to use the techniques. These parts delve into nuanced aspects of social interactions and self-awareness that could be challenging for a 9 -or 10-year-old's cognitive and emotional development level. For these parts, adult supervision is recommended to help younger readers navigate these concepts effectively.

Introduction Letter to Children

Hey there!

Have you ever had the feeling that people know things you don't? There you are, living your life, trying to get through your school, and you get the sense that you're missing something. You want to make new friends, but for some reason, it feels awkward. Or, perhaps you would prefer not to be so argumentative and get into so many misunderstandings, but you don't know why it keeps happening. What gives? There is a high chance that you need a social skills toolkit to save you from this problem.

In life, you can't help but interact with others around you. If you want to live most of your days without having a headache because you don't know how to connect with people, you need this book. So, how would you like to make communication your superpower? What would it be like to always know the right thing to say at the right time? Think of the difficult people in your life. Can you imagine being able to handle them like it's *no big deal*? Picture yourself taking on bullies with confidence, making them think twice about getting in your face again. Imagine having friends and family so close that nothing could get between you. These things are possible, and when you read this book to the end, you will experience these and more.

There's a catch, though. You have to put everything you learn in this book to work. It may not sound like fun right now, but by the time you become really good at these social skills, you will be the most magnetic, charming person in the room nine times out of ten. You'll no longer have to feel awkward for just existing. Finally, when you become a grown-up, these skills will help you like nothing else will at work and in many other ways, so it's better to learn them now than later. If you doubt that, ask your parents why social skills matter. They'll probably have some interesting stories to share that will convince you to read this book three times over as if your life depended on it. To be honest, your life does depend on how well you socialize. So, are you ready to become a master of everything social? You know what to do. Head to the next page right away.

Chapter 1: Speaking Your Mind

Have you ever wondered what life would be like if you didn't talk to anyone? Well, picture that for a moment. You don't say anything to anyone — not your parents or friends. Not only that, but you have no other way of letting them know what you're thinking, and you can't share your thoughts. So, no one can tell what you need from them, and you can't help them if they want something from you in the first place. You can't share ideas. You're just locked in your head. In this imaginary world, even sign language and gestures aren't allowed. You may be thinking this would be a terrible and impossible world to live in, and you'd be right. That's because, one way or another, you have to communicate with the people around you. Even when walking down a busy sidewalk, you communicate with other strangers without using words. Did you know that? It's true. How else can you tell when you should get out of someone's way when they're in a hurry?

So, what is communication, really? It's not just about talking. If you think it is, here's another world to imagine. In this one, everyone talks, but no one listens. It's an entire universe of moving lips but ears that don't exist. That would be a weird place to be in, right? Now, how about a different world where everyone talks and hears, but no one's actually *listening*? You could say to someone, "I'd like to have a diet soda," and they heard the words coming out of your mouth, but they didn't get it. For all they know, you could have said, "I would like to plant a cockroach."

Communication is a two-way street.
https://pixabay.com/photos/girls-friends-relaxing-lifestyle-7326492/

Interestingly, you live in a world like this. You could tell someone, "I would like some space and time to myself because I need to clear my head," and they'd assume you meant, "I really don't want you around because I don't like you." Thankfully, some people are great at listening and understanding. You can become one of them, too, now that you know what communication is about. Communication is about passing a message to someone else in a way that makes it impossible for them to misunderstand what you mean. It's also about receiving feedback from them about the message you shared without mistaking what they meant for something else. *Communication is a two-way street.*

How Communication Affects Relationships

Now that you know what communication is and why it's so important, it's time to understand what relationships are. Think about the word "relationship" and where it comes from. That's right. It's from the word "relate." When you "relate" with someone or something, you find that there are things you share with that person or thing.

The people you relate with are those who have something in common with you, even if you're both arguing with each other. How? Well, you both have the thing you're arguing about in common. For instance, your friend may think Veggies Tales and Southpark are both fine for your five-year-old little sister to watch, but you feel they are different. What on earth do you and the other person have in common, then? After all, you don't agree with each other. Well, in that example, you both have your passion for television shows in common. You're relating with each other about which genre is appropriate for little brothers and sisters –and the only way you can do that is through communication.

Do you feel awkward sometimes when you're talking to others? If yes, then when you learn how to communicate with others, you'll shed that feeling of being out of place. Think about the friends you have right now. You know, the friends you feel at home with. How did you become friends? Well, you had to communicate with each other. Now, think about the most recent argument you had with someone. Or, have you somehow never argued a day in your life? Then, think about the last time you saw two people in a heated disagreement with each other, whether in real life or in a movie. Now, ask yourself, why did their argument get to the point where they were calling each other names, yelling, or walking away from each other rudely? It's because there was a breakdown in how they communicated their points of view with each other.

So, you see, if you want to maintain great relationships with your family, friends, and the sweet old man in the store across the street, then improving your communication skills is a fantastic thing to do. You deserve to congratulate yourself for reading this book and learning how to connect with others around you. Some of the adults who should know better don't know half of the stuff you will discover. That's quite the flex, so . . . good job!

When people don't know how to communicate, they pass along their message to others in funny ways that just don't work. In the process, they get the opposite of what they wanted or come across as manipulative. For instance, they could go around the place slamming doors instead of letting someone know they're upset by what they did or said. Or, they could pick a fight about who touched the thermostat when what they really want to say is they were hurt by something you told them. Sometimes, they'll shut down and refuse to engage with you. It's not always because they're *trying to be mean.* They just *don't know how* to express their feelings because they never learned healthy ways to do so, like you're about to. Next thing you know, the relationships they have with the people around them are ruined.

What Communication Is About

Three important things make communication possible: The sender, the message, and the receiver. The sender is the person who starts the communication process by sharing the message they have with the receiver, who is the person the message is meant for. There is more to communication than these three components, though. When you communicate with someone, there's a three-step process.

1. **Encoding**: First, you have to encode your message. What does this mean? You're putting the message together, figuring out the best way to phrase what you want to say. Encoding also involves working out the right tone of voice to use and other aspects of communication that don't involve the actual words you're sharing.

2. **Channel**: Now that you've crafted your message, you have to think about how to pass it on to the receiver. Are you going to tell them? Would you rather write to them? Or do you want to forget about words and communicate with your body language? Whatever you settle on is the channel you're choosing to work with.

3. **Decoding**: Finally, you've sent your message, and the receiver has it. Now, they have to unpack what you've shared to understand what you're trying to share with them. If they do this right, the communication process is complete and successful. Suppose they think you wanted them to feed their imaginary pet monkey when you really wanted them to pass the salt! In that case, something has gone horribly wrong with the process. Maybe the wind blew a little too strong, so your friend couldn't catch your words. Or, there could have been some other form of noise that interfered with your message, causing the receiver to wonder why on earth you'd think they had a pet monkey — and an imaginary one, at that.

Types of Communication

- Verbal communication

- Nonverbal communication

- Written communication

You're smart, so you can tell the difference between each method, but here's an explanation of each communication type so there's no confusion here.

Verbal Communication: When you say the words, "I want to talk to you," you're using verbal communication because you're speaking words aloud.

Nonverbal Communication: When you raise your hand in class because you have a question to ask the teacher, that's nonverbal communication. Why? You didn't use words, but you used a sign or a gesture that both you and the teacher know — one that says, "I have something to say, but I'd like you to tell me it's okay to speak first before I do." Nonverbal communication works with your body language, facial expressions, and gestures. So, give someone a wink, a wave, or a smile, and you're using nonverbal communication.

Written Communication: Finally, there's written communication. You're using written communication when you send a text or write a note to someone.

Communicating to Express Yourself

Have you ever thought about acting? It's fun to play a different character than who you are, don't you think? Now, imagine a life where you have to act all the time. You need to pretend to be someone else 24 hours a day, seven days a week, for all of your life. That doesn't sound like fun anymore, does it? It would be exhausting. Unless you want to become a method actor — an actor who believes they're really the character they're playing while the camera's on them — there's no reason to be anyone but yourself. When you can express your true self freely, you'll enjoy a life free from stress. You won't have to worry about being seen as "fake" or wonder when someone will notice you're being phony. Also, people can trust you because they know the real you. What does this mean? The relationships you have with others will be terrific. There's only one way to express who you really are: through communication.

You'll have no trouble letting your true colors shine when you know how to communicate your thoughts and feelings. You become someone others can trust because you have no trouble being yourself, and you're always the same. Does this mean you'll never upset people? No, it doesn't. In fact, being true to yourself means you'll step on some toes sometimes, but they'll realize your honesty is something they can appreciate and lean on. They'll know you as someone who won't keep things from them. This quality of expressing yourself is called authenticity, and it's a magnet for attracting great friends and keeping people who are toxic away from you.

Expressing yourself means sharing the things you love and not taking part in things you don't care for. For instance, someone may think singing is lame, but you don't let what they think keep you from your school's Glee Club because you enjoy singing with others. If they say, "Wow, Glee Club is full of losers, isn't it?" you won't agree with them because you want to be true to yourself. You express yourself honestly by saying, "Well, I don't think so. I love it, and I'm signing up." The person judging the club may think you're lame, but because you're being honest about how you feel, others who share your passion for singing will know you could be a great friend. So, you see, communication isn't only about words and gestures — it's also about how you present yourself to the world. Be yourself, and you'll draw people who enjoy you just as you are while avoiding the headache of being misunderstood when you pretend to be who you're not.

Assertiveness, Aggressiveness, and Passiveness

When you're being assertive, you're not afraid to share what's *really* on your mind. If you don't like the lasagna you're having for dinner because it's salty, you say so. It doesn't mean you talk to others rudely. Rather, you're honest about how you feel and don't let others talk you out of your ideas or thoughts about anything. Assertiveness involves letting people know you prefer this over that. You allow others to share their wants with you, too. You respect what they have to say, but if you have a different opinion, you express yourself with confidence. For instance, if your friends want to hang out at a certain spot, but you're enjoying a fun video game at home, you can say, "Hey, I'd really love to stay home and play that game instead."

Sometimes, people get so worried about their voices not being heard. They worry someone will mow down their opinions, so they act bossy to stop that from happening. In other words, these people are being aggressive in their communication. If you choose to be like them, you'd say, "We're all going to stay at my house and play games, and that's the end of that!" You don't let others have their say, and you don't care about what they want. Communicating like this feels forceful, and your friends will feel like you are pushing them around. This isn't fun for them; if you keep it up, they may stop spending time with you.

Finally, you can be passive when you communicate. However, just because you can be passive doesn't mean you should. What does passiveness look like? You don't let others know what you're thinking. You really would love to have fun at home by yourself, but you let your friends steamroll you by going along with their decision to hang out elsewhere. You don't speak up for yourself. Now, there are times when it's okay to be chill and passive like this, but be warned: If you're always letting others have their way, you won't have fun. You'd be inauthentic, and as you've already learned, that can be exhausting.

You now know it pays to be assertive rather than passive or aggressive. So, how can you communicate with assertiveness?

1. **Be positive when you're speaking.** Decide that even when you're disagreeing with someone, you'll be positive in how you word your feelings. So, you could say, "I was hoping we could have fun playing this new game I got today." That's much better than just saying, "I don't want to go out." You're being upbeat about it, and by saying "we," you include your friends in your excitement about your idea.

2. **Be clear when you speak.** If you're vague as you speak, then there's no way others will understand what you want. So, be clear. Now, assume your friends have agreed to stay at your place, but they want to play a different game. A vague thing to say would be, "I guess we can play the other game, then." You know that's not what you want, and you know that sentence sounds like you don't mind when you really do. So, instead, be clear. "I want to play this one because I just bought it, and I read it's amazing."

3. **Listen to others.** Listening isn't about waiting for them to finish talking so you can say your piece. It's about paying attention. You pay attention when someone else speaks

because you're offering them respect. You wouldn't like it if you were sharing your ideas with someone and they weren't listening to you, would you? So, offer them that same respect. You could say, "I want to play this one because I've seen the gameplay on YouTube, and it's really awesome. I think you'll like it, too. Would you like to see it so you can see what I mean?"

4. **Use "I" statements as you speak.** If you say things like, "You always choose what we should do," your friends may feel attacked. Also, it's not true that people "always" or "never" do something, so that's not a fair thing to say. Instead, talk about how you feel and what you think by using "I" statements instead. Look at the statements in the previous tips, and you'll notice you're speaking for yourself, not for others.

5. **Practice being assertive.** Take every chance you get to speak assertively to your friends and family. Assertiveness is a muscle. Work it out, and it will become stronger. Have you always been passive? In the beginning, being assertive will feel scary, but the more you do it, the more you'll find there's nothing to fear. It will become normal for you. Are you usually aggressive? In that case, by practicing assertion instead of aggression when you communicate, you'll find more and more ways to say what you think and feel in ways that don't push people away.

How to Be a Good Listener

Remember, listening is a key part of communicating. If you listen, you'll know what the other person's saying and the best way to respond to them while respecting your feelings and theirs. Use these tips to develop the superpower of active listening, and watch how your friendships and relationships become even more awesome.

1. **Maintain good eye contact.** If you want to really listen to someone, keep your eyes on theirs. Not only does this help you focus your attention on what they're sharing with you, but it tells them you value what they're saying. The great thing about this is they're more likely to listen to you, too, to return the favor.

2. **Pay attention to what they're not saying.** In addition to the words coming out of their mouth, you can also pick up on their emotions. Try this fun exercise: Think about the

phrase, "I want ice cream." Now, does that sound like the speaker is excited about ice cream? What if they're angry, sad, or bored? In your mind, you're probably hearing that sentence in different ways. You can try saying the phrase aloud yourself using various emotions. Cool, right? So, the next time you listen to someone, notice their tone and emotions.

3. **Ask questions.** Think of yourself as a detective or a researcher. You want to learn more about what they're sharing with you. The next time your friend tells you something, you can ask, "How did you feel about that?" or "What happened next?" These questions will help you understand the other person better.

4. **Show them you get them.** If you are the kind of person who is supportive, always cheering others on and showing them you understand them, people will love interacting with you. You could say, "I get where you're coming from," or "Wow, that sounds amazing." Statements like this warm the other person's heart. Only say what you mean, though.

How to Use Nonverbal Communication

1. **Use your face.** You can communicate with your expressions. Is someone sharing good news? Smile to show them you're happy for them. Are they sharing something deep? A serious look or a studious frown while holding their eyes with yours shows them you understand them. As you use your face, you should also notice what the other person is doing with theirs.

2. **Use body language.** A big hug tells the other person you're comforting them or happy to see them, depending on the context. Drumming your fingers on the table as someone speaks could mean you're bored, and keeping your arms folded across your chest could mean you're defensive or challenging the person speaking to you, so be mindful of things like that. You are talking all the time, not just with your voice, but with your body. When you notice how people use body language when they feel one way or another, you'll learn a thing or two about what to do with yours.

3. **Notice pauses.** Sometimes, a long pause says more than words could. A pause could mean anything, depending on the context. If a friend wants to tell you something but pauses, it could be because they feel uncomfortable. So, you can reassure them by either encouraging them to speak or by asking, "Is everything okay? Do you want to talk about it?"

4. **Follow your instincts.** Have you ever noticed someone looking sad? You ask them what's wrong, and they tell you they're fine, but their face and body language say that's not true. In times like these, it's best to trust your instincts. You could tell them, "You may not want to talk about it now, but when you're ready, I'm here to listen, okay?"

To close this chapter, here's a golden nugget to remember: When you connect with others, you should be open-minded and empathetic. When you're open-minded, you think flexibly. You may not agree with everything someone says, but you are willing to hear them out.

For instance, if your favorite ice cream flavor is strawberry, but someone else prefers chocolate, it wouldn't be open-minded of you to say, "Strawberry is better than chocolate." Instead, you'd recognize that chocolate is just as awesome, too, at least to this other person.

What's another superpower for picking up on things the other person isn't saying? It's empathy, which is understanding how other people feel. Empathy allows you to respond in a good way when someone's feeling down. It tells the other person you get what they're going through and that you care about them. Later in this book, you'll learn how to sharpen your empathy, but first, you need to know about emotions.

Chapter 2: The Emotional Rollercoaster

Emotions are interesting. One moment, you're up. The next, you're down, and after that, you're "meh." What gives? You're human. It's natural to feel different things at different times. In this chapter, you'll understand your emotions, why they fluctuate, and how you can handle them like a pro so they don't get the better of you.

The older you get, the more interesting emotional experiences you'll have. Now, "interesting" doesn't mean it's always going to be fun times ahead, but the beautiful thing about these experiences is they'll allow you to grow and discover more about yourself. Do you think you know everything there is to know about you? Guess again. As time passes, your emotions will teach you new things about yourself. The cool part about these lessons you get is you'll become even better because of them. That's right — even the "yucky" emotions can be good if you let them.

Your emotions will teach you new things about yourself.

The Basics of Emotional Awareness

Do you want to win the game of life? Then, you have to understand the basics of the feelings you have within yourself. When you are aware of your emotions, it's easier for you to communicate with others. Why do you have to be aware of your emotions? Well, for one thing, your emotions are a big part of how you talk to other people. They determine the way you connect with them. Imagine being upset about something that happened at home. Someone chooses that moment to ask you for your assistance with their math homework because they don't understand a problem. Usually, you're cool about helping out, but this time, you sharply tell them to take a hike. You wonder why you lashed out at your friend the way you did in response to the request. This isn't the first time they've asked you to explain things to them.

So, why are you now losing your head, you wonder? It's because you weren't aware of how you were feeling. It didn't occur to you when you shifted from a positive or a neutral mood to a bad one. Also, you haven't realized you can unfairly transfer your anger or pain to others when your feelings are all over the place. You weren't mad at your friend. You transferred your feelings from whatever upset you at home to them, *which wasn't fair.* You know that. How can you keep that from happening again?

When you keep track of your emotions, it's easier for you to make the best decisions for yourself. You know when it's a good time to take a chance on something and when to hold off. Why? If you're not feeling great, your bad mood could make you do something you'd regret later. You understand yourself by studying what's happening inside your head and heart. As an added bonus, your mental health will be amazing.

Many people struggle with messy minds, but you won't have to worry about that because you know what to do when you're not feeling your best. Does emotional awareness mean feeling good all the time? Absolutely not. As much as you may want to stay happy forever, that's not possible. Your emotions will go up and down. This is normal, especially normal for a young, growing person like you. So, don't feel like you're a failure for being unable to hit the gold standard of emotions. There's no such thing. It's all about balance.

Hormones and Mood Swings

Your body is incredible. If you could see its inner workings, you'd think of it as a lab where a set of special scientists conducts all sorts of cool experiments. Who are they? They're hormones. They move around your body, carrying messages back and forth to tell it what to do. Your hormones are the reason for the changes you notice in your body as you become a grown-up. Have you realized your voice is getting deeper? Are you growing taller? Is hair showing up in all sorts of weird places? Well, you can thank your hormones for doing their job.

Sometimes, hormones get a little too active. You'll know because you feel like your emotions are all over the place. In one moment, you're happy and over the moon. In the next moment, you're moody and wondering if you'd like an emo wardrobe to express the darkness in your heart. Who can you blame for this rollercoaster? Well, look no further than your hormones. They're responsible for messing with the console that controls your emotions, and when you don't step in, they can get out of hand sometimes.

As you become a teenager and then an adult, your body will change. There's no way to stop the process because it's natural and it happens to everyone. In the meantime, you'll feel awkward in your own skin. That awkwardness can feel like you're in the wrong body or the wrong life, but if you ask any responsible adult, they'll tell you the truth: The awkwardness is only a phase. It will pass, so don't freak out too much, okay?

Now, as these changes are happening, your brain has some new work to do. How on earth does it handle this storm of emotions? It has more complicated work to do, and you'll have to help it. The changes you're going through will affect how you connect with your friends and family. Some days, you're more sensitive than usual and want to be left alone. On other days, you're fine with socializing. Either way, these mood swings you experience are normal and part of growing up. Now, the question is, how can you help your brain handle your feelings?

Knowing and Naming Your Feelings

Sometimes, you feel great, and other times, you feel terrible. Which emotion is which? In this section, you'll learn the precise names of the ways of feeling you usually have.

Positive Emotions: When you feel good, you are experiencing a positive emotion. Here's a look at what they are:

1. **Joy:** Happy feeling. You're glad to be alive, to be with the people you love, and you are in love with your life in this moment. When you're joyful, you smile and laugh easily.

2. **Love:** A strong feeling. When you love someone, you feel warm and fuzzy while thinking about them or being with them. You feel like you don't want to be anywhere else. If it's something you love, you treat it like treasure. Love also makes you feel safe and relaxed.

3. **Surprise:** When something happens that you could have never expected, you're surprised. That's the feeling you get when your parents get you something you thought they never would. It's also possible to be surprised when something bad happens, but in this context, this is a *pleasant* surprise.

4. **Pride:** Think of something you're really good at. It could be something you've made, like a class project. That warm feeling in your chest when you've done something

everyone is congratulating you for is *pride.* You feel satisfied and pleased. You could be proud of something you've done, something you have, or who you are.

5. **Relief:** Have you ever done something you shouldn't have? It could have been a total mistake. Or maybe you were feeling rebellious and naughty, so you did something you knew you shouldn't have. Now, you're worried about getting in trouble. However, when you find out it wasn't a big deal, or an adult tells you it's okay, you feel like the balloon in your chest is now deflated. You breathe more freely. That feeling is called relief. It's the urge to say "Phew!" and wipe the sweat on your forehead.

Negative Emotions: It's time to talk about the not-so-great emotions. They're not great only because they don't feel nice, not because feeling them makes you a bad person. Remember, everyone feels them, and it's okay.

1. **Anger:** When you're annoyed with someone or something, you're angry. You don't want to be around them. Sometimes, you'd rather not think about the thing. You may feel like screaming or hitting something when you feel anger. Your heart beats faster, and you feel ready to run.

2. **Sadness:** When you're sad, it's because you've lost something or someone. It could also be because something you'd hoped would happen isn't going to. Sadness makes you cry. You feel empty and all alone.

3. **Fear:** You know how you feel when you sense danger? That's fear. You feel afraid when you think you may get hurt somehow. When you're afraid, your heart also beats fast, and your body can tremble.

4. **Disgust:** When something irritates you, you're disgusted. You can't stand that thing. You don't like it and don't want to be around it. You don't understand why it should even *be a thing* to begin with. You can also feel disgust for people.

5. **Shame:** Remember a time when you did something you realized you shouldn't have? The feeling after is called shame. You want to run and hide from everyone. You wish the floor could open up and swallow you, or you could become invisible at will. That's how shame makes you feel.

It's okay to feel all these emotions, both positive and negative. In fact, it's a sign that your mind is healthy when you feel all these feelings. You should become familiar with these emotions. How? As you stop what you're doing to do a different thing, ask yourself, "How am I feeling right now?" The more you do this, the more you'll figure your emotions out. You'll also be able to tell what happened to make you feel the way you did, and that's a good thing.

Your Triggers

What are the things that can change the way you feel or make your mood swing from low to high and back?

1. Your mood changes depending on what's happening to you at the moment. If you lose a game, you feel sad or angry. If you try something new and you enjoy yourself, you feel happy. These personal experiences will always affect your feelings.

2. The way you feel also changes depending on the world around you. For instance, when the rain is falling, and the sun is nowhere to be found, you may feel down. If it's your birthday, you're happy. If you have a big test coming up, you feel afraid.

3. Other people can also make you feel things. When talking with your family, friends, or even strangers, you can feel all kinds of emotions, depending on who they are to you and what you're both talking about.

4. Social media can affect your mood. Remember Facebook? It's operated by Meta now. Once, they took part in a terrible experiment where they showed 689,003 people posts that would make them sad or angry in order to see how it would affect them. It worked. So, you should be careful about what you watch and how much time you spend online because it can affect your mood.

5. Your body can make you feel different things, too. You may act out or not want to engage with anyone when you're hungry. When you're tired, you can feel less happy about life. So, check in with your body when you're tracking your mood.

Now that you know the many things that can trigger you, how can you know what's causing you to feel the way you do?

1. **Keep a diary.** In this diary, write down everything you did during your day, how you felt about each event, and why you felt the way you did. Do this every day, and you'll find interesting things about yourself to help you feel better, even when your emotions are negative.

2. **Before you do anything, ask yourself how you feel.** When you're done with that activity, ask yourself how you feel once more. Keep doing this as you switch from one thing to another.

3. **Notice how you feel when talking with someone, and then ask yourself how you feel afterward.** For instance, you may have had a good time with a friend, but then you both disagreed about something and now you're upset. It's good to track that. Why? You'll know you should only feel that way about the disagreement and not take out your anger on someone else. You'll also keep yourself from doing the next activity with anger and having another bad experience.

4. **When you watch a movie or a video and cry or play a game and become frustrated with the level, notice these things and write them down in your journal.** Then, write about why you felt that way, and see how you can manage the feeling better the next time you feel that way. Maybe you could give social media a break for a bit or remind yourself that failing a video game level doesn't make you a bad person or ruin your life.

5. **Pay attention to your body.** Are you feeling grumpy? Well, see if you need a nap or if you're hungry. Are you feeling stressed or anxious? Moving your body could help. You'd be surprised that you'll feel better when you give your body what it's asking for.

How to Cope with Emotions

Use these tools whenever your emotions feel too much for you to bear:

1. **Breathe deeply.** Find somewhere quiet, take a deep breath in through your nose for four seconds, then hold it for four seconds. Next, breathe out through your mouth for four more seconds. Keep doing this, and you'll calm down.

2. **Write in your journal.** When you share your feelings with your diary, you empty them out of your head and heart and onto the page. You'll feel light again.

3. **Talk to someone you love and trust.** You can tell this person how you feel; they'll understand and support you. You don't have to deal with emotions on your own. So, reach out to a friend, a teacher, or someone in your family who can hear you out.

4. **Switch your thoughts around.** When you catch yourself thinking, "It's no use," or "I'll never get this right," or "I hate this," you can replace those thoughts with something that feels better. For instance, you could say, "Well, I can try again," or, "It's okay if I don't get this right now. I'm still learning."

5. **Take a break.** If you're doing something that's frustrating you, you can walk away and come back to it later. Is it a tough conversation you're having with someone? Tell them you'd like a moment to calm down and reset, and then you'd be happy to talk about it with a cooler, clearer head later.

6. **Use Threes.** What does that mean? Look for three things you can see, touch three things around you, listen for three sounds you can identify, notice three things you can smell, and if you're eating, pick out three flavors you can identify. This mindfulness technique will settle your mind and help you handle your emotions better.

So, now that you know how to ride the rollercoaster of emotions you experience every day... what's next? It's time to understand yourself and know why you act the way you do.

Chapter 3: Introvert, Extrovert, Ambivert

Do you know your personality type? When you know the kind of person you are, you'll know what you need out of life. You'll only take part in the stuff that makes you happy. Have you ever seen some adults who go to work and always come back home miserable? One reason could be that they're working a job that doesn't fit their personality type.

When you learn who you are, you'll know the kind of work you should go for and what you should avoid. Whatever you do, *don't skip this chapter*! When you share what you learn from here, you will help others understand why you act the way you do. Your friends and family will have a better connection with you when they know who you are. Plus, you'll be able to figure out their personality types to improve your relationships with them. Think of this chapter as the cheat code of human behavior.

Extroversion - Ambiversion - Introversion

Preference for **more** stimulating environments

Preference for **less** stimulating environments

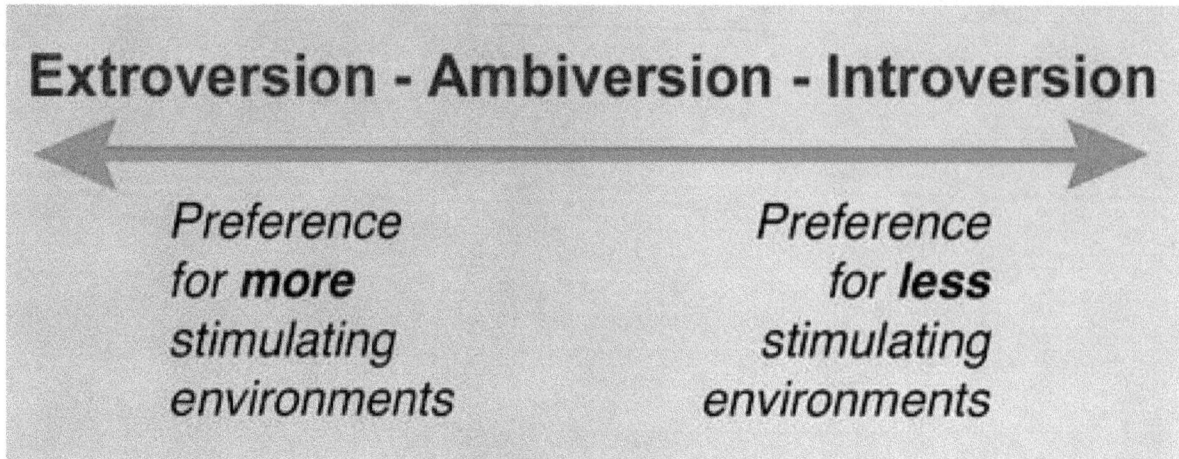

Get to know your personality type.

Three Kinds of People

There are three kinds of people in the world. Okay, you probably looked around and thought to yourself, "There is no way there are only three kinds of people in the world." You're right. The point is you can put people into three major groups. What are they?

1. Introverts

2. Extroverts

3. Ambiverts

The Introvert: How can you tell an introvert apart from everyone else? If you look around your class during recess and you find that one person who's hunched over a book in the back of the class or somewhere secluded, the odds are that person is an introvert.

Everyone else can be chatting and having fun, but they're not really into it. Is this you? If you are an introvert, nothing gives you more joy than being by yourself. You love the kinds of activities that don't require too many people or anyone at all, if possible. Having to spend time in large groups can feel draining to you.

You read a lot or watch movies by yourself, too. You're always in your head because the thoughts you have are far more fascinating to you than what's happening outside. It would take something extraordinary to pull you out of your amazing imagination. It is in your imagination that you come up with the most extraordinary, out-of-this-world ideas – and everyone loves you for it.

The Extrovert: Do you know someone who's always the center of attention? They love to hang out with other people. They always seem to know the right thing to say at the right time. These people are extroverts, and they are the social butterflies of the world.

Nothing gives them more energy than spending time around other people and interacting with them. They not only love to party, but they are also the life of the party. If you want someone who is great at connecting with other people, look no further than the extrovert.

If this is you, you are amazing with your friends. It's thanks to you that the introvert has some sort of a social life. Introverts tend to get "adopted" by extroverts (and while they probably won't tell you, they're thankful that you exist, dear extrovert). As an extrovert, you wear your heart on your sleeve. It's not difficult to tell what you're feeling at any point in time. People feel comfortable approaching you if they have questions or if they need some help.

The Ambivert: Can you see introverted and extroverted traits in yourself? Guess what? You're an *ambivert*. You have a really cool superpower that allows you to shapeshift as needed. You feel just as comfortable in a room by yourself or in the middle of a big party. Your shapeshifting ability means you enjoy spending time by yourself just as much as you enjoy socializing.

For you, it's all about finding balance. This is a great thing because you can be an excellent friend who hangs out often and also know when it's time to go back into your shell and recharge yourself. It all depends on your mood.

Struggling to remember which "vert" is which? Check out the table below so you can always remember.

	You're an Introvert if...	You're an extrovert if...	You're an ambivert if...
How you recharge	You'd rather be alone	You love to be in groups	You're fine alone and fine with others
How you socialize	You prefer small groups or one-on-one connections	You love parties, and you'll show up for any gathering	You can handle one-on-one interactions and all groups, small or large
Your superpower	You're a master of your mind and exploring things alone	You're the life of the party everywhere you go	You're a shapeshifter, at peace with being social or solo

Remember how it occurred to you that there must be more than three kinds of people? You're right. That's because you need to consider personality types as a spectrum. Think of frozen water as one end of the spectrum and hot water as the other. The frozen water will eventually melt if you don't leave it in the freezer, right?

As the water melts, it loses its coolness and becomes room temperature. You may think of this room temperature as being warm. Now, if you put that water in a kettle and boil it, it would go from warm to hot. Also, when you think about it, you realize that what's warm to you is cool to another. Where does warm even start? In the same way, people can be anywhere from introverted to extroverted. Not every introvert is always quiet, and not every extrovert is always outgoing.

The Introvert's Strengths

You're a great listener. Whenever people talk to you, they feel like they've really been heard. That's because you truly have heard them. You're not only listening to what they're saying, but you're also paying attention to how they *feel.*

You're a thoughtful person. You think a lot, and you think deeply. You don't know how **not** to think. You enjoy chewing on ideas in your mind, turning them this way and that in order to understand them on a deeper level than most people bother with.

You have no trouble being alone. This isn't only in social contexts but also when you have an idea that other people don't agree with. You have no problem being your own cheerleader. From the outside looking in, people may think you are bored being alone. However, they have no idea how much of a blast you're having in your head.

The Introvert's Challenges

You are drained by crowds. If you were Superman, crowds would be your kryptonite. You can't stand to be around too many people for too long, and when you get back home, you feel as if all your life has been sucked out of you.

You won't find it easy to meet new people. This challenge is the reason why you may not have much of a social life. It's not like you're complaining, of course. The few people who know you and who you've allowed into your life are more than enough for you. However, it doesn't hurt to let in some more people.

You have a hard time expressing your thoughts. What's fascinating about this challenge is you have the most brilliant ideas. However, when people want you to say something in a conversation that's moving too fast within a group, you don't do well with that. You need time to organize your thoughts so everyone understands what you're saying.

Strategies for the Introvert

Always prepare first. Do you have somewhere to be? Do you have to give a speech or talk to other people? In that case, you could take time to rehearse. You'll feel more comfortable when you're there.

Take short breaks when you're hanging out with groups. You can take 5 minutes to recover in the bathroom or some quieter place at the venue. This way, you're ready for the next round of socializing.

Use writing or art to express yourself. You can always write them a message whenever you don't have the words to tell someone what you feel. You can even use art if you prefer.

The Extrovert's Strengths

You breathe life into every room you're in. You're so energetic because you are surrounded by other people, and you love that. The people you're with can feel your excitement. Just by being there and being yourself, you make it a fun time for everyone.

You're a great team player. You love working with others and get along fine with most people. Thanks to you, everyone can get coordinated and do what they need to do to finish a project. You're like the glue that holds it all together. When you grow up, you'll be that one person in the office who always knows what to say to a difficult boss or client.

You're an excellent communicator. As the saying goes, you have the "gift of gab." Nobody can quite word things the way you do. Also, you have no trouble allowing your thoughts to flow freely.

The Extrovert's Challenges

Sometimes, you get a little too excited. There are certain situations where your bubbly, bouncy energy may not be the best. So, learn how to read the room and find balance in your energy levels.

You like to hog the spotlight. You're not doing this on purpose. You're just wired that way. Others who don't understand you're an extrovert may think you're trying too hard for attention. You have to learn to share the stage with others.

You feel drained when you can't socialize. You feel down if you don't get enough energy from other people. You must find ways to interact with others as often as possible.

Strategies for the Extrovert

Learn how to balance your energy. There won't always be a party, and you won't always have access to people, so learn how to stay excited in times like these. Find activities and hobbies you enjoy, and you should have no problem with this challenge.

Be as inclusive as you can. What does that mean? Give other people a chance to shine the way you do. Sometimes, they may be a little shy, and they'll never get the chance to speak if you don't let them. It doesn't hurt if you use your extrovert superpower to coax them out of their shell and into the spotlight.

Learn to listen more. The only thing better than a fun extrovert is one who has both ears open and pays attention to what people tell them. When you hear people out, they'll love you all the more for it.

The Ambivert's Strengths

You're a flexible person. You don't have trouble enjoying groups and different situations. You're at home either talking with one person or mingling with millions. Well, maybe not millions, but you get the point. Crowds don't scare you.

You work well on your own and with groups. Your introverted side, thoughtful and creative, will be very useful to the groups you work with because of the ideas you'll come up with. Your extroverted side makes it easy to share those ideas with others.

You are a great speaker and a great listener. You've blended the best of both worlds into your beautiful personality. People feel like you get them when they speak to you, and when it's your turn to say something, they're in awe of what you have to share because it's often helpful and practical.

The Ambivert's Challenges

Finding the sweet spot between solo time and social time can be tricky. You sometimes struggle by leaning too hard one way than the other. You may feel burned out when you don't find the balance between your introversion and extroversion.

You have trouble making decisions. Should you go out with your friends? Should you stay home and enjoy your new fantasy novels instead? You and your friends have been talking about checking out that new cafe that opened up in town, but those books are calling your name. What do you do? These are the kinds of decisions you struggle with.

You may struggle with your many commitments. You're the kind of person who says yes to most invitations. Why wouldn't you be? People love you. So, what's the problem? You spread yourself too thin, which can be too much to bear.

Strategies for the Ambivert

Create a schedule. You should assign certain times or days for hanging out with others and have special periods for yourself alone. With an actual schedule, you'll find balance and won't feel like you're being pulled in different directions.

Think of the pros and cons. When you want to make decisions, get a pen and paper and write all the upsides and downsides of each option you're considering. With this list, it will become easier to see what you prefer, and you'll make the right call for you.

Rank your commitments. When you sort them out in the order of what matters more or what's more fun, you'll immediately know what's worth your time. Do the things at the top of the list and handle the rest later.

For Your Introverted Side: Balance Being Social and Self-Care

1. **Make time that's strictly for you and no one else.** During this time, you can do whatever you want, whether it is reading, enjoying music, playing games, or creating something. You can tell the people in your life that you value your private time so they know not to bother you.

2. **Pick friends who get you.** You won't enjoy being friends with people who have trouble with you wanting to be on your own. True friends will understand you're an introvert and you can't do without alone time.

3. **Learn how to say no.** No is a good word. If you're invited out but have to recharge, say no. A good friend won't hold it against you. The more you learn to say no to things you

don't want to do, the better your boundaries will be.

4. **When you choose to hang out, be deliberate about it.** What does that mean? Before leaving home, decide how long you'll be at the event, and plan to take breaks while you're there. If you do this, you won't feel as overwhelmed during gatherings. You may actually enjoy yourself.

For Your Extroverted Side: Avoid Burnout and Maintain Healthy Relationships

1. **Make time for activities with your friends that will allow you to become even closer.** Think about things you can do with just one other person. By bonding with one person over something like a fun project, you'll have a stronger bond with them than if you flit from person to person all the time.

2. **Even extroverts need to take a break from all that socializing.** As fun as it is to connect with others, you should schedule some downtime when you can unwind and relax by yourself. Sure, you may think that's boring, but if you give it a shot, you'll be glad you did.

3. **Try exploring the world by yourself.** Is there some new place you want to check out? See what it's like to go on your own rather than with your group of friends. True – you get a chance to meet others, but you also learn about who you are outside of your friend group.

4. **Choose friends who love your extroversion.** These friends love that you're always down to hang out, and they'll appreciate your need to be around others. Does this mean you can't be friends with an introvert? You can, but if you want friends who are always down to go out, other extroverted people are the best kind.

No matter your personality trait, whether you're an introvert, an extrovert, or an ambivert (somewhere in the middle of the spectrum), you have your own unique superpowers. Love yourself as you are, and don't judge yourself for not being like someone else. This note goes especially to the introvert. If that's you, you've probably heard too many times that you should "loosen up more" even when you're feeling happy. If anyone is uncomfortable with you, that's their problem.

No matter what personality type you are, love yourself as you are. Also, don't judge others for being different from you. Everyone has something they're better at than everyone else, so celebrate those differences. With that out of the way, how would you like to make friendship a little less awkward? Flip to the next chapter to learn more.

Chapter 4: Making and Keeping Friends

So, do you want the secret sauce to making the best friends who fit you beautifully? Do you want to know how to hold on to those friendships for life? Well, this chapter will teach you all that and more. There are certain friendship principles that, once you master them, will give you the best of friends for the rest of your life. It's all about learning to create friendships full of love and positivity. These are the friendships that last — the ones that are healthy and supportive. When you know these special principles, you'll know how to turn a stranger into a great friend and keep them in your life. Add the other skills you're picking up from this book, and you'll find no one has more rock-solid friendships than you do.

It's all about learning to create friendships full of love and positivity.

The Value of Friendships

Can you imagine living without friends? Okay, if you're an introvert, you probably smirked and thought, yes, you can. Still, even introverts have friends, right? Friends are awesome. Did something awesome happen to you? A friend can celebrate with you, making your good news feel even sweeter. Are you going through something that is saddening? Your friends are people you can lean on until you get back up on your feet. There's nothing like having a crew of super people you can share all your feelings with in good times and in bad.

So, why should you start and grow friendships with people who match your vibe? The beautiful thing about having friends is they can help you grow. Friends will expose you to new things you might never have experienced if you'd been alone. They know stuff you don't, just as you know things they don't. When you get together, you share what you learn and help each other out of your comfort zone. This way, you all grow together.

Think about it. You could have a friend who's into music, and you're more interested in books. If they share their hobby of making music with you, you could surprise yourself by finding you're talented at making music. If you love books and share those with your friends, they may discover a love for reading, thanks to you. What are other reasons why strong benefits are great for you?

1. **Your friends will be there for you as you grow older.** When you experience challenging times in life, you can trust them to support you, give you advice when you're feeling confused, and help you see ways to improve your life.

2. **The friends you have now can be a part of your professional network when you are old enough.** Even when you are in different careers, you might find these connections with them useful.

3. **When you have great friends, your mental health stays excellent.** You have people to support you when you're down and people to turn to when you need company.

4. **Keeping friends and investing in them will help you become a more empathetic person.** You'll also have better communication skills than people who don't have as many friends as you do. You'll know what to do when there's trouble with difficult people and others don't know how to smooth things over.

Basic Friendship Principles

Certain building blocks make a good, true friendship. What are they?

Trust: Think of your head and heart as a chest full of treasures. These treasures are secrets you don't share with anyone, such as the things you're afraid of and your dreams. This treasure chest is trust, and you only hand over the key to people who are close and have shown you they care. You can't have a friendship where you and the other person don't trust each other. You build trust with your friends when you make promises and keep them. You show up for each other when the other person needs you, being careful about each other's feelings in how you say and do things. This trust makes your friendship impossible to break.

Respect: Friendships are built on respect. When you and your friend respect each other, you recognize you're diffcrent in certain ways, and you don't judge the other person for their choices. You treat your friends the way you expect them to treat you. For instance, if you don't like it when someone makes a mess in your room, you won't do this to your friends. If they know you don't like your workout session interrupted, they won't get in the way of it. If you lend them money, a true friend will pay it back when they said they would, or at least let you know if they can't pay it back when you agreed.

Support: Good friends cheer each other on. You're there for each other in highs and lows, showing each other you're not alone. Supportive friends are great because, as it turns out, sports players aren't the only ones who could use cheering. As you play the game of life, knowing you have people on your side feels good and can help you succeed.

Kindness: Friends are kind to each other. How? You know your friend has been talking about how they've been stressed lately, so you look for ways to make their life easier. They notice you're hungry, so they bring you some food when they visit. You are kind to each other in these little ways, strengthening your bond.

Communication: Communication is a big part of friendships. If you and your friends don't stay in touch, before you know it, you'll feel so distant from each other that talking becomes awkward. Also, you have to be mindful of what you say and how you say it so you don't hurt each other with your words.

So, ask yourself how you can be a better friend by seeing how you can work with these principles. Also, you'll know your friend's a keeper when you consider whether they treat you with these principles each time you're together.

Boundaries

Everyone has limits. You can only do so many things to be kind and supportive before you feel drained; this is why you should speak up when someone disrespects your boundaries. When you tell them, and they keep doing the same thing, you know you shouldn't keep that friendship. Boundaries are so important because they help you remain your true self. If you don't have boundaries or know where to draw the line, you'll wake up one day and find you can't recognize yourself. You'll notice you are a collection of what everyone else wants from you. Instead of letting things get so far that you lose yourself, you should have boundaries.

Think of your boundaries like broccoli. You may not be a fan of vegetables, but you have to get some in you so your body can work as well as it should, right? Well, it's the same with having boundaries. It may not be pleasant to tell someone they're crossing the line with you or that you have limits you would like them to respect, but it will do wonders for the quality of friendships and connections you'll enjoy.

No two people are the same, meaning everyone will want something different from you. If you don't have firm boundaries in place, you'll feel like you're being pulled apart. Boundaries will keep you from going crazy with figuring out who you should honor. They'll help you see what you need, what your friends need, and how to tell what's more important in different situations. They'll help you remember to stay true to yourself. You're probably wondering how to let someone know your boundaries without sounding rude or insensitive. Follow these steps.

First, you have to know your boundaries. You can take 5 to 10 minutes to write in your journal about what makes you feel comfortable and what you don't like to do. How do you feel about your time and space? What about your emotions? Are you the kind who doesn't appreciate people being too close physically? How would you prefer to be spoken to? These are the kinds of questions you need to ask and answer. As you figure out these things, you will know your boundaries.

Next, be clear about your boundaries. When you recognize them, let your friends know what they are. Is there something a particular friend keeps doing to you that they probably don't think is a big deal but bothers you a lot? This is a good time to let them know. Be direct and clear When telling your friends about your limits. Does this mean you should be rude? That's not necessary. You can calmly explain to them that you really enjoy your time together as friends and you would like for the friendship to keep growing. However, for things to stay good between the two of you, you would like them to respect your boundaries. You could even go a step further by asking them if they have any similar problems they'd like to share with you so you, too, can respect whatever limits they have.

Finally, be consistent. You're not being consistent if you communicate with others about your boundaries but allow them to keep acting toward you in ways you don't like. You're sending them a message that it's okay for them to keep treating you how they were, and if they aren't good people, they'll continue to disrespect you. Don't forget that you also owe your friends and family respect. If you know they aren't okay with certain things, you shouldn't do them. When you and your friends respect each other's boundaries, you deepen the trust you share. Your bond grows so strong it's like Gorilla glue. Nothing could keep you apart from each other.

Sometimes, people will make mistakes. You'll know if it's a genuine mistake because they'll do what they can to correct themselves, and they don't have a problem apologizing to you. In the same way, you should be quick to apologize to your friends if you break their boundaries. Always ask them questions if you're unsure if they're okay with something, and listen actively when they answer.

So, how do boundaries work in real life? Suppose your buddy would like to spend some time with you, but you'd rather study because you have a test coming up the next day. You could tell them, "It would be fun to hang out, but I need to get ready for tomorrow's test. How about we hang out during the weekend instead?" When you respond this way to your friend's request to have fun, you assert your boundary, which is that you need to use your time to study, and you also show them your respect for their feelings by offering to spend some time with them later on.

Here's another example. So, you really got this boundary business down. Do you have a friend who's always borrowing your stuff without telling you? You could tell them, "Hey, I noticed you keep taking my things, and you don't tell me about it. I'm fine with sharing, but please ask me first next time you want something, okay?" You've told them you have a boundary, which is that you'd rather be asked first before someone takes your things. You've also let them know it's okay for you to share your stuff with them as long as they let you know before they take it.

Making Friends

You don't have to sit in a corner and wait for someone to come and talk to you. You can always be the one to start a conversation. Yes, even if you are an introvert. How do you interact with others when you're in a new space you're unfamiliar with or see someone you think is interesting and want to get to know?

- **Always lead with a smile**. Usually, if someone is kind, they will smile back, and that's an invitation for you to go over and say hello. Your smile also lets them know that you're easy to talk with.

- **Start the conversation with an open-ended question**. What's an open-ended question, you ask? That is an open-ended question. In other words, it's the kind of question you can't just answer with a simple yes or no. It's the sort of question that, when asked, makes the other person say a lot more than a word or two. The more they have to say, the more questions you have to ask. For instance, you could ask them what they spend their time doing on the weekends or what they thought about the last movie they saw.

- **Share**. It would be weird if you just peppered the other person with questions. It would quickly feel like you're an FBI agent and, at any point, you're going to arrest them. They'll avoid you. So, share something about yourself, too. When you do, you help the other person feel at home talking to you.

- **As you listen and talk, look for things you both like**. When you have hobbies or other interests that you share with this other person, it could be a great way to keep hanging out with them.

- **Don't try to be someone you're not**. You're excellent the way you are. If the other person doesn't like something about you, that's their problem. You can always end the conversation politely and move on to the next person.

- **Keep practicing.** Not every conversation you have with a new person is going to be successful, so be okay with that. Some people are simply not open to friendships. Others are. You'll never know if you quit on the first try because that person was cold or standoffish. So, shrug it off and try again.

Usually, when someone is rude or unresponsive to you, it's not about you. They're struggling with it on the inside, even if they think or claim you're the problem. So, you don't have to take on that guilt or feel ashamed for being rejected.

Here is an important thing to remember before ending this chapter. You won't always turn every conversation into a deep friendship. There's nothing wrong with that. So, don't expect too much from someone you only just met. If you want a strong friendship with someone, both of you have to be equally interested and put in the work. Also, it's going to take time to develop the kind of friend that lasts a lifetime.

Chapter 5: How to Resolve Differences

No matter how much you love your friends, and they love you back, there will be times when you have to deal with conflicts. Sure, you are friends with people who have common interests and values, but that does not mean there won't be disagreements now and then. Knowing how communication should work and doing your best to communicate clearly does not mean there won't be misunderstandings.

Instead of letting these conflicts ruin your friendship forever, you can do something about them. Conflict resolution is a powerful social skill that will help you in your personal life and is necessary for humanity to thrive and succeed.

If everyone were mad at each other and not one person on the planet knew how to resolve problems, the world would be a bigger mess than it looks right now. So, how would you like to be a conflict-resolving superhero? How would you like to slice and dice your way through differences like a hot knife running through butter? You'll become a disagreement-busting Jedi master by the end of this chapter.

Conflict resolution is a powerful social skill that will help you in your personal life and is necessary for humanity to thrive and succeed.

https://pixabay.com/photos/girlfriends-friendship-hug-trust-2213259/

Conflict Resolution Principles

Conflict resolution, like communication, has its building blocks. If you don't consider these principles, you will fail when you try to resolve the difference between you and others. What are these principles?

Principle #1: Be buddies, not enemies. When you and your friend don't see eye to eye, remember you are a team. What's your goal as a team? You want to score positive points for your friendship, and that means figuring things out together. It's tempting to drift apart silently, but instead, remind your friends that you're not against them and would like to work out the problem together. For you to do this, you have to separate the person from the problem.

As buddies, you treat each other the way you would like to be treated. So, if you or someone else is being blamed for a problem, you can say, "I'm not the problem, and neither are you. The problem is this situation. If we work on it together, we can fix it."

It's like when you and your sibling would like to watch the TV at the same time, but you're interested in a different show. Rather than be frustrated with each other, you could work as a team to figure out something. You know, the problem is not the other person, but the fact that there's only one TV and there are two of you. So, what can you do? Maybe together, you can create a schedule for who gets to watch TV and when.

Principle #2: Be respectful. The thing about disagreements is that keeping cool is pretty tough. You've probably noticed this yourself, haven't you? When you are upset, it's hard not to say something you would regret later. You must teach yourself to control your urge to say something rude or hurtful.

By reminding yourself that this other person matters to you and that you wouldn't like to be spoken to rudely, it becomes easier to restrain yourself and show respect as you talk through the problem. If the other person does not treat you with the same respect, you could tell them that you will walk away from the conversation and that they can pick it up with you when they're feeling better.

Keeping yourself from saying anything hurtful doesn't mean you have to sit there and take it when someone else is being disrespectful to you. Let them know you don't appreciate their tone and that you'll end the conversation if they don't stop being rude or cruel.

Principle #3: Wear your shoes, and wear theirs, too. In other words, you should pause to think about how the other person feels about the disagreement. By doing this, you'll find that no one wants to feel bad on purpose, and they don't want this to linger. You can also see how what you did about the problem makes them feel.

For instance, if you borrowed a dress from a friend without asking (which you now know you shouldn't do), do you know what's better than just saying, "I'm sorry?" You could say, "I'm really sorry. I didn't ask you first, and I should have done that. It won't happen again. How can we work this out?"

Principle #4: Engage instead of tuning out. You know that's a really good idea. Way before you and your friend ever have a disagreement, you could both agree that whenever you don't see eye to eye, or you're upset with each other, you're going to talk it out. This way, the next time you disagree with each other, you don't fall into the trap of tuning each other out, which could cause your friendship to end. Instead, you can both have a seat, talk about how you feel, and listen to the other person.

Avoiding problems is for cowards, and you're no coward, are you? Of course not. Avoiding each other doesn't make the problem go away. You can't pretend it doesn't exist, and you shouldn't. Even if it seems like you're both okay now because no one brought it up, be brave and speak with your friend about the problem. Why? You never know what's going on in someone else's head. You may think you're in the clear, but that problem may be all they can think about, and it would only be a matter of time before they drift away from you.

Principle #5: Accept your part instead of blaming them. When your friendship hits a bump in the road, it's tempting to blame the other person. You think to yourself, "If only they'd done this instead of that, things wouldn't be like this right now." Here's the thing, though. There are two people in a friendship, which means there are two people responsible for what's happening.

You can't keep pointing fingers at your friend without thinking about what part you played in causing the rift between you. So, do a little detective work to see how you may have gone wrong or what you could have done that you think is right, but the other person doesn't. How do you do this? Check out principle #3. You can go a step further by talking to a neutral third party about it and asking them how you may have gone wrong. When you figure it out, you can disclose this to your friend. They'll feel like you understand them, and they'll be more willing to smooth things over.

Principle #6: Keep your cool. Disagreements can get heated. Tempers and nostrils flare, no one's listening, and each person wants to have the last word. That's no way to keep your friendship or resolve things. Whether it's with a friend or a family member, you have to stay cool and not allow your emotions to get in the way. It's about more than holding your tongue. Remember, your body talks, too.

When you're keeping a calm head, you don't sigh, roll your eyes, tap your foot, cross your arms in front of you, or do anything else that would make the other person more upset than they already are. You know this is wrong, but how can you keep from doing it? Immediately when you notice you're about to explode, breathe deeper and longer, making sure you empty your lungs completely each time you breathe out. If you can, ask for a break, and promise you'll come back to talk about your issues when you've had a chance to cool off. Then, go for a walk, listen to music, take a nap, or work out to let go of your anger.

Negotiating Like a Boss

Would you like to know how to negotiate with friends and family during difficult disagreements so everyone walks away happy with one another because there's a solution that works?

Use your ears before you use your mouth. Your goal is to understand. How? Listen to the other person first. Give them a chance to get it all off their chest. They may say things that make you feel the urge to cut in, but place an imaginary padlock on your lips and keep them locked until you know they're done. When it seems like they are done, don't just start talking. Instead, ask, "Is there something more you want to say? If there is, you can. Understanding you matters to me, and I promise to listen no matter how hard it is to say it." Then, do just that if they have more. If not, then you may share your thoughts.

Meet each other in the middle. Can you suggest different ways you could compromise? If you're short of ideas, you can ask them for their help. When you do, you could phrase it this way: "I'm out of ideas for how we can fix this. What do you think could help us right now? Got any ideas?" By inviting them to think of solutions, they warm up, and you can come to an agreement that leaves both of you happy. Compromise isn't about you grudgingly accepting something that doesn't work for you. It's working out a solution that both sides will be content with. So, work together to brainstorm ideas that could work. Remember, you want to compromise, not one-up each other.

Please use "I" statements. Have you ever heard someone accuse someone else of being a narcissist because they always say "I"? Well, you can ignore that because that's not how it works in negotiation and disagreement. Pretend your family member or friend says to you, "You make me feel so angry and frustrated." How does that feel? Not very good, right? It feels like a kick in the teeth.

Now, pretend they say this instead. "I feel so angry and frustrated." Do you see the difference? The first example blames you for their feelings, and if you didn't know better, you'd think you were a problem and try to avoid them. In the second sentence, they're sharing how they feel, so you can empathize with them. Next time you have a disagreement with someone, use the word "I" generously. Avoid "you" statements unless you're saying something positive or supportive. Even when it's something the other person did wrong, you could say, "I noticed you did this the other day," or "I felt really bad when you didn't pay me back my money when you said you would."

Remain friendly. Did you know being angry or sad doesn't keep you from being kind and open with the person who hurt or upset you? You can be really mad at someone and still remember you love them. When you know this, it's freeing. If you've ever seen two friends at each other's throats because they're angry with each other, you now know that's not the way to go.

Want to try something interesting? The next time you're angry or disagreeing with your friend or family member, try giving them a warm hug or gently holding their hand while looking into their eyes, and softly tell them, "Hey, I'm really upset with you right now, but I care about you, and I want us to fix this." You'd be surprised to find you don't feel like blowing your lid, and they'll be so shocked that they'd be willing to sort things out as soon as possible because of how cool you're being about things.

Chapter 6: Strengthening Family Bonds

Family matters. Not only is that the name of a 90s sitcom, but it also *really does*. How you relate with your family will determine whether you're happy at home – or not. Think of your family as a mini society, where everyone has to play their part to protect and be there for one another. When you have strong family ties, you'll enjoy your life. These people will be there to support you emotionally, even when there's no one else. Your family is your rock, loving you and being there for you throughout your life.

When you have strong family ties, you'll enjoy your life.
https://pixabay.com/photos/family-african-american-happy-7257182/

Family Roles

Some people aren't fortunate enough to have every member of their family present with them. Sometimes, that's because their family members have passed on to the other side, they didn't grow up with them or they had a terrible background. In cases like these, people choose others who are not connected to them by blood and think of them as family. If you are fortunate enough to have your biological family with you and are generally having a good time with them, you should celebrate that. There's no better way to show your family you appreciate them than to know their roles in giving you somewhere to call home.

Parents: Your parents act as your support. They are your primary guides. They are the leaders of the pack. Do you have any trouble? They're the first people you should turn to. Are you trying to figure out the best decisions to make, but you're feeling confused? You can trust your parents to help you figure things out. They'll keep you safe from as many challenges as they can manage, but the way life is set up, something difficult will happen now and then that they can't keep you from experiencing. Does that make them terrible people? Absolutely not. As great parents, they'll be there to support you through whatever you're experiencing until you come out on the other side with a smile on your face.

Siblings: Think of your siblings as playmates for life. They are your partners. They are awesome because they can become excellent friends, and you can share things with them. They'll understand you inside and out in ways that other people outside your home may not. Every now and then, you'll argue about whose turn it is with the television, but the fact remains that they are the ones you can rely on through thick and thin, and they're a good time, too. Also, you may want to talk about things you are afraid to bring to your parents. In this case, having siblings you can share with first is lovely.

Grandparents: Your grandparents may be old, but that's no reason to look down on them. They are full of wisdom that can help you. They've experienced so much in life, and they can share the lessons that they've learned, so you don't have to make the same mistakes they did. They also have some of the most fascinating secrets regarding your family. Curious about your family's history? You should be. You should have conversations with your grandparents. No one knows the fun stuff better than they do.

Aunts and Uncles: Your aunts and uncles are also part of the family. You can think of them as a different version of your parents. There's so much you can learn from them, too.

When you have a strong family to lean upon, it makes life easier to handle. Every member will experience their highs and lows, but the family unit is there to support them through it all. Even when things appear tough and scary, knowing that you are not alone is a refreshing, reassuring thought. What's not to love about being in a family? You can enjoy unconditional love even when you're not at your best. You learn so much about how the world works from your family members, and there is laughter and fun in each lesson. You create precious memories together as you go on holidays and other adventures. You create a story that will remain in your mind forever.

Practical Tips for Communicating with Family

You love your family, don't you? So . . . if you care about the bond you share with these awesome people, you'll want to communicate with them in ways that allow you to remain close to one another. So, here are some tips to help you with that.

Decide you'll be a super listener. Aren't superpowers cool? It would be nice if you could melt metal with a laser from your eyes or teleport from your home to outer space in a second. Since these superpowers aren't possible (at least not in this universe), choose to become so good at listening that you could be a superhero. Remember, listening is important in communicating well with others. Give your family your full attention when they speak. Hear what they're saying and notice what they're not saying. Show them you care by repeating what they've shared with you and asking if you understood them. If they say you didn't, ask them to explain again, and be patient.

Share your feelings. Being a super listener shouldn't mean you never get the chance to share. When you have something on your mind, share it with your relatives. Do you sometimes think to yourself, "What I think doesn't matter," or "This feels too heavy, and I don't want to bother them with this?" Please bother them. They're your family. Who else are you supposed to lean on if you can't share with them or your friends? By sharing, you remove the huge load from your back and show your family you love and trust them enough to support you however they can. It's nice for them to know that, so share.

Pick the right time to engage with them. When you want to tell family about something important, ask yourself if *it's the right time.* For instance, suppose you and your family enjoy movie night at 8 PM on Thursdays. It's a time for everyone to relax and have fun. That's not the best time to bring up a serious matter, is it? You could wait for the movie to be over and for everyone to calm down before you begin talking about what you want to share.

Remain kind, even when the truth hurts. Your family is human (right?), which means they will do things that aren't always nice. When you want to confront them about these things, you can tell them the truth while being kind. Remember, "I" statements are better than "you" statements.

Respect their feelings and thoughts. You're a tribe, but that doesn't mean you all think the same way. Even when they have thoughts that are way different than yours, or you can't relate to the way they feel about something, still show them you respect them. How? Allow them to share their ideas. Ask them questions to understand their point of view better. Wanting to understand doesn't mean you have to agree, but it shows that you care and value them.

Bonding with Family

You should want to spend time with your family. The more time you spend with the people who love you, the stronger your connection will grow. Do you know what else is awesome about having a strong bond with your family? It's the fact that it makes it easier to communicate with each other because you'll know each other better. Here are some ideas for how you can bond if you're not already using them.

1. Make family game night a weekly thing.
2. Cook as a family. Make breakfast or dinner together routinely, and it will surely bring you closer.
3. Go out together for things like picnics, bike rides, or sightseeing.

4. Have a movie night once a week or every couple of weeks when you all watch several movies or binge episodes of a great TV show.

5. Make some music together. It doesn't have to be professional. You don't need a studio, and you don't need fancy equipment. You can clap, sing, hum, whistle, and come up with tunes and funny lyrics on the spot about whatever you want.

What other activities can you think of that would allow you and your family to bond? Make a list of your own. You can bring it up with them and have them contribute ideas, too. No matter what activities you settle on, you'll be glad you have time to dedicate to one another. Bonding time like this will help you become more empathetic and kind toward the people you share your home with, and that's a very good thing.

Chapter 7: Peer Pressure and Other Struggles

Now, it's time to talk about something uncomfortable: Peer pressure. Have you ever been in a situation where you had to deal with someone who doesn't take no for an answer? They want you to do something you really would rather not. It feels even worse when there's more than one person because you suspect they think you're no fun for not going along with their plans. They say anything to get you to cave and go along with what they want.

It's tough dealing with difficult people and situations, isn't it? Well, there's no magic age at which people stop trying to pressure you into things. So, learning how to deal with that pressure is important, and the sooner you master this skill, the better. This way, even as an adult, you'll know how to stand firm and only do what you believe in. You won't make decisions because someone else is putting the squeeze on you. Instead, you'll be your own person, unafraid to be the only one on your side.

Learning how to deal with that pressure is important, and the sooner you master this skill, the better.
https://pixabay.com/photos/stop-sign-traffic-sign-road-sign-634941/

What Is Peer Pressure?

Peer pressure is when your friends or peers force you to do something. Sometimes, what they want you to do could be good for you, and other times, it may not. Peer pressure could either be forceful and obvious or subtle. When you're experiencing peer pressure, you are being influenced by others.

There are two kinds of peer pressure: Positive peer pressure and negative peer pressure. When peer pressure is positive, it's a good thing. It means your friends are encouraging you to do the right things. They want to see you win. Maybe you've been having trouble motivating yourself to take care of something or start a new project. In that case, your friends can be there to cheer you on.

On the other hand, peer pressure can be negative. This is when you're being pushed by your friends or mates to do things that aren't right or that don't feel good to you. For instance, you may know it's wrong for you to skip class, but they feel you should join them and go to the mall or a party instead. Or, your friend may be drinking something they shouldn't and trying to make you have some.

There are three main forms that peer pressure can take on, whether positive or negative. What are they?

Direct peer pressure: Have you ever been in a situation where your friend is talking you into something? They say something like, "Come on, just do it. Everyone's doing it. Why won't you?" That form of influence is called direct peer pressure.

Indirect peer pressure: Now, you may be thinking to yourself, "I have good friends, and no one is making me do things I don't want to." That may be the case, but not always. You can be pressured into acting in certain ways without anyone saying a word. How is that possible? Everyone around may be engaged in something, and even if they don't say anything about it, they act like you're a weirdo for not wanting to join in. That feeling is uncomfortable if you don't know your boundaries and haven't practiced saying no. So, you may be silently roped into their schemes without them needing to say anything to you. That's indirect peer pressure. Their body language tells you all you need to know: "Join us, or you're not one of us."

Self-imposed peer pressure: Have you ever looked around you and felt the urge to fit in with everyone else? Maybe you're in a new environment that you've never been in before, and you don't recognize anyone, but you can see they have certain habits that may not be great. So, the thought enters your head that maybe if you do what they're doing, you will be accepted, and people will like you more. You fall in line because "When in Rome . . . "

Spotting Peer Pressure

There are different ways that you can experience peer pressure. Here's a look at some of them.

1. You want to dress the same way your friends do so you don't feel like you look weird.

2. The only reason you play sports is because your friends do, too . . . not because you care for it.

3. If you have friends with strong opinions and loud voices, you go along with whatever decisions they make, even if you wouldn't choose what they did.

4. When you scroll through social media, you notice how everyone looks cool and like they're having a good time, so you feel the need to post a few videos of your own to seem the same as them, even if you know you aren't.

How to Resist Unwanted Peer Pressure

Some peer pressure can benefit you if you're driven to do the right thing. However, what do you do when someone tries to get you to do something that is against your instincts or morals?

First, know who you are and stay true to that. Ask yourself what you want out of life to figure out your authentic self. What are the things that matter to you? Do you care about honesty, kindness, and respect? How about trust? Is loyalty something you value? Or, being a good person? Take five to 10 minutes to write what matters to you in your journal. Then, read through what you've written, and you will begin knowing who you are. When you know who you are and what you stand for, it's immediately obvious when your friends are trying to get you to do something that is not you. By figuring out your values like this, you can also learn and stick to your boundaries, staying true to yourself.

Next, always check in with yourself. Whenever someone tells you to do something, and you feel uneasy about it, don't just remain in the feeling. You can take a break by telling this person you'll discuss the topic with them later and then check in with yourself. How do you feel about what they're suggesting? Why do you feel that way? When you write down how you feel, you'll know for a fact that you don't want to do what they're asking of you, and it's easier to put your foot down and tell them no. Of course, if what they're asking is an obvious red flag, don't give them the idea that you'll come around to their point of view later. Your response should be a firm no as you look them square in the eyes.

Grow your "no" muscle. When you work out, your muscles get bigger, and you get stronger. In the same way, when you practice saying no consistently, you'll get better at it. With each no, you'll sound more confident. You don't care if someone calls you names or tries to make you feel silly. You're "no" stays no. There's no talking you out of your decision.

"No" is an excellent word that protects you from dangerous things and people. So, start practicing it and learn to be okay with the icky feeling of facing off with people who don't know how to take no for an answer. You can practice doing that in a mirror if you don't get enough chances to say no in real life. You can also share this knowledge with a friend and practice with them.

Promise yourself you will never make decisions on the spur of the moment. Don't wait until you're in an uncomfortable situation to decide. Do it now. Put this book down, find a mirror, look yourself dead in the eyes, and as you point at your reflection, say, "I promise you (your name here); I'll never decide too fast without thinking things through just because someone's pressuring me."

The next time someone tries to get you to do something, take a break from them. If it comes to something more forceful, tell them you have to use the bathroom; then, when you're away from them, make a list of the pros and cons of doing what they want. Something about looking at that list immediately helps you see whether you want to be involved in what they're inviting you to do or not.

Have a code word you share with your friends and family. Whenever someone is pressing too hard, you can say this word, and your friend or family will know to rescue you from them. Think of it like a bat signal or the red button you can push to call in the troops to save you.

Be picky about who you are friends with. Remember the section about boundaries? Well, a true friend would recognize that you have certain lines that shouldn't be crossed. So, if they're trying to get you to cross those lines, that's not a good friend.

Let a responsible adult you trust know about what's going on. There are certain situations where it's easier to involve a grown-up. This is the case when you're dealing with a bully or some other difficult person. The moment you realize this isn't something you can handle on your own, speak to your parents or any other adult in your life who is always there for you.

School Stress and Social Stress

1. **You can't beat stress.** It's unavoidable. It's everywhere you go. So, the question is, how can you manage it? Whether it's related to schoolwork or your social life, you will always experience the challenge of stress, so the best thing to do is learn what tools you can use to handle it. Fortunately for you, you're about to learn them right now.

2. **Use your breath to ground yourself.** Anytime you're feeling too stressed out, and there's tension in your neck and shoulders, you can take a deep breath in as slowly as you can. Hold on to that breath for a few seconds, and then exhale. Do this several times, and it'll feel like cool water pouring over your soul.

3. **Manage your time better.** How can you do this? First, make a list of everything that you do in life. What does your average day look like? When you have it all down on paper, ask yourself if there's anything on that list that isn't necessary. Cross those things off your list. Now, you're left with what's important. Next, create a schedule so you know how long it should take you to do your tasks. Does it feel like you have too much to do? You can break down each thing on your list into smaller steps so it feels like you can pull it off.

4. **As you move from one activity to the next, pause to check in with yourself.** Ask yourself how you're feeling. If you notice you're not feeling so great, ask yourself what you could do to feel some relief. Is it something you can't do right away? Comfort yourself with the fact that you'll eventually have time to do that thing. Let that thought give you the strength you need to withstand the stressful situation you're facing right now. You've got this.

5. **Always do the most important thing on your list first.**

6. **Take breaks before you break.** What does that mean? Why wait for your body and mind to send you distress signals and tell you they will shut down if you don't shut them down? Instead, *get ahead of the stress.* How? You should schedule breaks into your daily activities. Breaks are good. They help you recharge and find the energy to keep going.

7. **Eat good food and get proper sleep.** You'd be surprised at how less stressed out you'll be.

Bullies and Confidence Issues

Sometimes, you may have to deal with a bully. How can you handle them like a pro? How do you keep them from pressuring you into doing things you don't want? How can you help someone else who is being bothered by them?

Speak up whenever you see bullying in action. It's not okay to just stand there and do nothing. You should always say something even if you don't know the person getting bullied. If the bully is someone you can't handle or talk down to, invite a grown-up to handle the situation.

Stay safe from online bullies by being careful with what you share. If you're getting bullied on the internet, you should report to an adult who can handle the situation. Also, don't waste time blocking that person and reporting them on the social media platform.

If someone's bullying you, you should say something to a grown-up. You don't have to carry it on your own. Think about at least one adult you can talk to who could come to your aid and put the bully in their place. Tell the school authorities about this bully, too.

The interesting thing about bullies is they have low self-esteem and no confidence in themselves. Since they don't know how to handle that truth, they turn and lash out at others they think are better than them. The way a bully treats you is a reflection of what they think of themselves. So, don't take it personally, no matter what a bully tells you. Instead, work on boosting your self-esteem and confidence. How can you do this?

1. **Make a list of everything that you love about yourself.** You can also ask trusted friends and family to tell you at least three good things about you and then write them down.

2. **Use positive affirmations to help you feel like a superhero. What** are those? They are awesome statements that you make about yourself. For example, you could say, "I am a strong, kind person," "I love and respect myself," or "I handle challenges with ease and grace." What affirmations can you come up with? Make up your own, and say them in the mirror first thing in the morning and last thing at night.

3. **Whenever a negative thought pops up in your head to make you feel bad, immediately replace it with a positive one.** The more you do this, the fewer negative thoughts will occur, and the next thing you know, your mind is constantly generating positivity.

4. **Love the fact that you are different.** There's never going to be anyone like you. Also, you can't be like other people, so celebrate that. The next time anyone tries to make you feel bad for being different in any way, you can tell them, "Yes, that's how I am, and

I'm okay with myself." Obviously, if they say something bad about you that isn't true, you should not be thanking them for that or accepting their hurtful words. Instead, walk away from the conversation like a boss. It drives bullies nuts when you show them they aren't getting to you.

Here's a final note before you head on to the next chapter. If you're ever dealing with a difficult situation or a difficult person, please find people who can support you. If they've made you feel uncomfortable about your body or anything else, you need to report them and get help to feel better. Don't be afraid to reach out to your friends and family. Connect with the adults around you so they can help you handle any challenge that you are facing. ***You don't have to be alone.***

Chapter 8: Social Success Toolbox: Further Skills

You made it all the way to the final chapter. You should be so proud of yourself. The fact that you've stuck it through to the end says that you will definitely kill it when it comes to your social skills! How would you like to become the ultimate boss when it comes to your social life? You're about to be equipped with the big guns of social skills. Armed with these, no one will stand a chance against you. People will love you for who you are, and you'll find yourself floating through different social situations like a ninja. How cool is that?

Remember that people will love you for who you are.

Advanced Empathy

Would you like to go a step beyond empathy? Would you like to understand someone else so well that you're almost inside their skin? Yes, that sounds a little bit creepy, but it is possible for you to understand and connect with someone like that. How? By using the process of empathy mapping. Here's how to do it:

Pick a target. Who is it that you'd like to connect with better? Who would you like to understand even more? This person will be the subject of your empathy mapping. You can choose your friend, someone in your family, or even a movie character if you want to.

Take a piece of paper and draw the map. Simply split the paper into four different sections of a square. Label each square as follows:

- Said

- Did

- Thought

- Felt

Write in the "said" section. What did this person say? Can you remember their words precisely? Write it all down in this section of your map.

Fill in the "did" section. You're going to write not only your target's actions but also the way they behave. Watch their body language and write down anything you can pick up on. What decisions did the person make? Write those down, too.

Write in the "thought" section. Obviously, there's no way for you to tell for sure what someone else is thinking, but you can't put yourself in their shoes and make guesses, either. Try to imagine you know what's going on in their head and write it down in this section of your map.

Now, fill in the "felt" section. Once more, there's no way you can read their mind, but when you put yourself in the other person's shoes, you can figure out how they could be feeling about things. Write down whatever your gut tells you.

Review your map. Now that every square is full of your observations, look at what you've written down. What can you tell about this person? What have you realized? Have you noticed something new that you missed before? Do you now see how it's possible you may have misjudged them? Make a separate note about what you've concluded about this person.

This is a beautiful process to use when you're dealing with people who are difficult or when you'd like to connect even better with someone else. Empathy mapping is not technically a science, but it's a great way to get a good read on people.

Digital Etiquette

You're probably using the internet a lot more than you used to. The internet is such a wonderful place because you can learn so many things! However, you need to be careful, just like in real life. It can be a jungle out there. Also, there are proper rules that you need to follow, just as you would in different settings in real life. So, if you want to stay safe on the internet and enjoy yourself in the process, these rules must be followed. Together, these rules make up digital etiquette, or, if you want to be fancy, "netiquette."

1. **Always interact with others respectfully.** There's no reason to be rude, even when you don't agree with them. It is easy to forget you are not just looking at words on a screen. Someone else is on the other side responsible for those words you're reading. So, be mindful of their feelings when you communicate with them.

2. **Think long and hard about whether you should post something before you do.** If you post this thing, is it possible that you'd hurt someone's feelings? If the answer is yes, then you shouldn't bother posting that.

3. **Protect your privacy.** You don't want to put all your business online because that's a great way to get yourself in trouble. It's sad, but not every human being is nice or kind. So, don't post your phone number, email address, or full name anywhere.

4. **Never share things without getting permission first.** If you and your friends took a photograph at an event and want to share it on your page, check with them to see if it's okay before posting it.

5. **Whenever you are joking or being sarcastic, be clear.** It's so easy to be misunderstood on the internet, so if you joke about something, you should say it's only in good fun and shouldn't be taken seriously.

6. **Respect people's opinions, even when you don't agree.** It's okay not to see things eye to eye. You didn't come into the world to be like everyone else, so you shouldn't expect others to agree with every word you say. You should also be kind and hear others without telling them they're wrong or making them feel stupid.

7. **Never spam.** No one likes a spammer. What's that? A person who sends the same message repeatedly. It's not cool.

8. **Spell your words correctly and use proper grammar.** Posting something on the internet differs from sending a text message to the people who know you and understand your codes. Write clearly so that others can understand you.

Teamwork

How would you like to work well with others and even have a good time doing so (especially you, introvert)? Teamwork is a useful skill to have in school, and later on when you have a career. Sometimes, you can achieve far more when you work with others than when you're alone. So, follow these tips, and you'll be golden:

If you have an idea or a question, share it with others. Don't be afraid to speak up.

1. **Be the kind of person who loves to cooperate.** What does that mean? You like working together with other people. Don't be afraid to share tasks and see how you can help others. If something feels too much for you, be open to letting someone else help you.

2. **Everybody on your team deserves your respect.** So, whenever they share an idea, you should hear them out. Show them that you value what they think. When they demonstrate skill at something, you should celebrate them. Always be kind to your teammates.

3. **Decide to be the kind of person they can rely on.** If you want to be successful while working with a team, you can't afford to let anyone down. Did you promise you were going to get a task finished? Then, do it. Everyone is trusting that you'll come through, so it's heartbreaking when you don't.

4. **Keep a positive, upbeat attitude.** There will be times when your team will experience challenging situations. It's tempting to give in to the negativity and say there's no point in trying. However, by staying positive, you help the rest of your team pull themselves up and give the project another go. Also, they'll learn this habit from you and consider you a great leader.

Respecting Differences

The world is a colorful and vibrant place full of all kinds of people. Everyone deserves respect. It doesn't matter what culture they have, what their background is, or what they believe in. You should always be willing to see the other person as another you. What does that mean? Treat them the way you would like to be treated.

Some people look at others who are very different from them and decide that is a reason to be disrespectful and cruel. This is terrible behavior that you should not engage in. It doesn't matter if someone is of a different race, ethnicity, religious belief, political belief, or ideology other than yours. They're allowed to be different. Here's how you can respect diversity and be more inclusive:

1. Do all you can to learn about other cultures.

2. Keep an open mind, even when someone has values and beliefs that are different from yours. You don't have to agree with them, but you can show them you respect them.

3. Avoid assuming you know people based on hurtful stereotypes about their culture or beliefs.

4. Whenever you see someone being discriminated against, say something. Speak up for the other person and tell the bully it's not okay to do what they're doing.

Social Etiquette

Life as a human means that there will be times when you have to be social, you have to go out to certain events, and you are expected to act in certain ways depending on where you are and who you are with. The following are useful basic social etiquette rules to follow.

1. The minute you do something wrong, apologize and ask how you can fix things.

2. It's better to ask for permission before you do something.

3. Are you in the middle of a conversation with someone? Don't look at your phone. Also, don't answer the phone if it rings while you're still talking to this person unless it's an emergency, of course.

4. It's good practice to keep eye contact as you are talking with others.

5. Did someone give you a gift? You should say thank you.

6. If you're invited to a party, a dinner, or some other gathering, always bring the host a gift.

7. When you're eating with others, don't speak when your mouth is full.

8. Don't stretch your hand across the table to reach for a condiment. If it's too far away, ask someone who's close to pass it to you, and they will.

9. Speaking of passing food, you should always pass from your left to your right.

10. If you have two mutual friends meeting each other for the first time, introduce them to each other.

11. If you're taking a walk with a friend and you are stopped by someone you know, don't stop to have a long conversation with this new person and leave your friend standing aimlessly. Introduce them to each other and keep the conversation with the person you ran into very short. After all, you're spending time with your friends, not with them.

12. Always wait your turn in the conversation before you speak. It's impolite to speak over someone or cut them off.

Upgrading Your Body Language Reading Skill

How would you like to be even better at reading body language than you already are? Here's how:

1. **Pay attention to the tone of their voice as they're talking to you.**

2. **Is your friend acting weird? Pay attention to the situation.** It could be because there's someone in the room they're unfamiliar with, or they are somewhere different from where you're used to seeing them, like at a party. So, as you read their body language, think about how the environment or event may have affected the person.

3. **When someone's talking to you, notice which words they emphasize.** As you do this, you'll learn a whole lot more than what they're saying.

4. **Pay attention to the eyes.** If someone's smiling at you with their lips but looks like their eyes are dead, that could tell you they're not really happy to see you. A real smile will often cause crinkles to form at the corners of their eyes.

5. **Watch the way other people interact with each other.** If you see that two people are closer to each other than others, that could tell you that they are good friends or there's something more going on. Also, when people like someone, they'll mirror what the

person is doing. So, see if you can spot that.

6. **Read books and watch videos about how to read body language.** The more you learn, the better you'll be at picking up on the subtle stuff.

Conclusion

You finally made it to the end of this book – Congratulations! You now know the importance of communicating effectively. You know how you should speak what you're saying and how you shouldn't. You understand so much, at least in your head. The next step is to take all you've learned and put it into action. Please take it easy on yourself. You're not going to learn every single thing in one day. Reading one book on how to develop your social skills is not enough. You have to keep learning through books and by going out and doing what you have read.

Think of developing your social skills as your life's work. The better you get at interacting with your family, friends, and strangers, the higher your chances of experiencing a happy life will be. Not only will you be satisfied, but with the connections you grow and keep, you'll also experience benefits in your professional life. You have a higher chance of succeeding when you know how to interact with people. Never make the mistake of thinking that your talent is enough to sell you to others or make them like you. You should also know how to present yourself to others, and this starts with putting these skills to work day after day.

At first, you may find it terrifying to do things you have never done. It may even feel unnatural to you initially, like setting boundaries, resolving conflicts, etc. Still, the more you practice, the better you'll get, and it will become second nature. You won't even have to think about these skills because you'll naturally use them wherever you are. You'll know how to adapt depending on where you find yourself or who you're talking with, and that is a really cool superpower.

Thank you so much for reading this book! Take everything that you've learned from these pages and put them to work. Then, watch as your relationships magically transform. You'll love connecting with people no matter where you are or who they are. Already, you've done such a great job reading to this point, which could only mean one thing. You are bound for social success. You're going a step further by acting on what you've learned. You are willing to put in the work, and that's why you will definitely be rewarded for it. So, once more, thank you for taking the time to read to this point, and you should also thank yourself for doing so!

Check out another book in the series

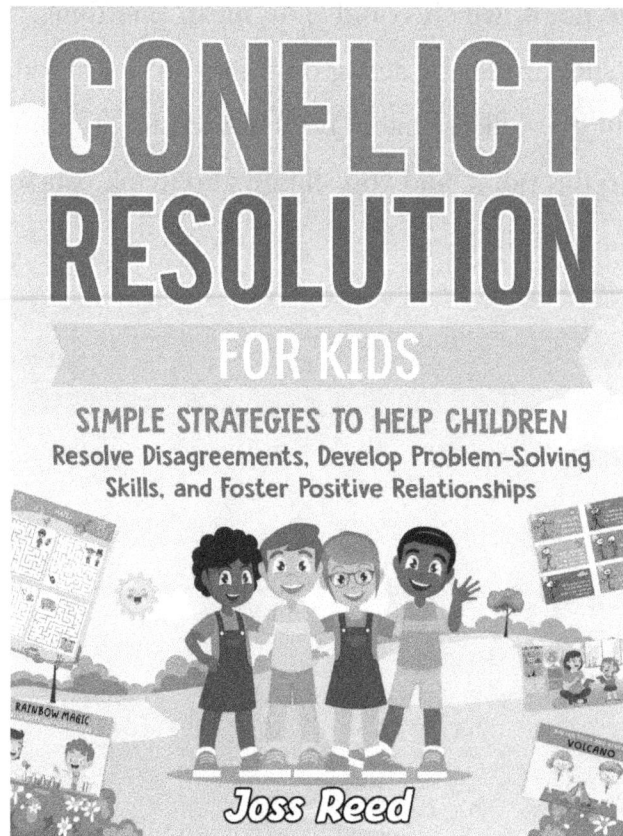

CONFLICT RESOLUTION FOR KIDS

SIMPLE STRATEGIES TO HELP CHILDREN
Resolve Disagreements, Develop Problem-Solving
Skills, and Foster Positive Relationships

Joss Reed

References

Combs, M. L., & Slaby, D. A. (1977). Social skills training with children. In Advances in Clinical Child Psychology: Volume 1. Boston, MA: Springer US.

Eisler, R. M., & Frederiksen, L. W. (1980). Perfecting social skills: a guide to interpersonal behavior development. Plenum Press.

Elliott, S. N., & Gresham, F. M. (1993). Social skills interventions for children. Behavior modification.

Evans, J., & Irving, D. (2001). Social skills. Scholastic.

Fitzsimons, K. (2021). The teen's guide to social skills: practical advice for building empathy, self-esteem, & confidence. Rockridge Press.

Gladdin, K. (2022). The social skills workbook for teens: exercises and tools for building empathy and boosting confidence. Rockridge Press.

Gresham, F. M. (2002). Best practices in social skills training. National Association of School Psychologists.

Hargie, O., Saunders, C., & Dickson, D. (1994). Social skills in interpersonal communication. Psychology Press.

Laugeson, E. A., & Frankel, F. (2011). Social Skills for Teenagers with Developmental and Autism Spectrum Disorders. Routledge.

Leutenberg, E. A., Butler, C., Brodsky, A. L., & Whole Person Press. (2014). Teens - social skill strategies: facilitator reproducible activities for groups and individuals. Whole Person.

Little, S. G., Swangler, J., & Akin-Little, A. (2017). Defining social skills. Handbook of social behavior and skills in children.

Merrell, K. W., & Gimpel, G. (2014). Social skills of children and adolescents: Conceptualization, assessment, treatment. Psychology Press.

Riggio, R. E., Throckmorton, B., & Depaola, S. (1990). Social skills and self-esteem. Personality and Individual Differences.

Singleton, W. T. (1984). Social skills. Mtp Press.

Walker, H. M. (1988). The Walker social skills curriculum: the ACCESS program, adolescent curriculum for communication and effective social skills. Pro-Ed.

Windell, J. (1999). Six Steps to an Emotionally Intelligent Teenager. Trade Paper Press

www.ingramcontent.com/pod-product-compliance
Lightning Source LLC
LaVergne TN
LVHW061328060426
835511LV00012B/1914